SACRED SPACE

for Advent and the Christmas Season 2014–2015

"The website *Sacred Space* has been helping millions to pray for some years. Now Ave Maria Press makes these very helpful and easily usable prayer-helps available in handsome and accessible form, including pocket-sized booklets for the Advent/Christmas and Lenten seasons. What a great service to God's people! I hope millions more will buy the books. God is being well served."

William A. Barry, S.J.
Author of *Paying Attention to God*

SACRED SPACE

for Advent and the Christmas Season 2014–2015

November 30, 2014, to January 4, 2015

from the website www.sacredspace.ie
Prayer from the Irish Jesuits

ave maria press AmP notre dame, indiana

Acknowledgment

The publisher would like to thank Brian Grogan, S.J., for his kind assistance in making this book possible. Correspondence with the Sacred Space team can be directed to feedback@sacredspace.ie where comments or suggestions related to the book or to www.sacredspace.ie will always be welcome.

Unless otherwise noted, the Scripture quotations contained herein are from the *New Revised Standard Version* of the Bible, copyright © 1989 by the Division of Christian Education of the National Council of the Churches of Christ in the United States of America. Used by permission. All rights reserved.

Advent retreat by Brian Grogan, S.J., used with permission.

Published under license from Michelle Anderson Publishing Pty Ltd., in Australia.

Founded in 1865, Ave Maria Press is a ministry of the United States Province of Holy Cross.

www.avemariapress.com

Paperback: ISBN-13 978-1-59471-556-3

E-book: ISBN-13 978-1-59471-557-0

Cover design by Andy Wagoner.

Text design by K. Hornyak Bonelli.

Printed and bound in the United States of America.

Contents

How to Use This Booklet

We invite you to make a sacred space in your day and spend ten minutes praying here and now, wherever you are, with the help of a prayer guide and scripture chosen specially for each day of Advent and the Christmas Season. Every place is a sacred space, so you may wish to have this book in your desk at work or available to be picked up and read at any time of the day, whilst traveling or on your bedside table, a park bench. . . . Remember that God is everywhere, all around us, constantly reaching out to us, even in the most unlikely situations. When we know this, and with a bit of practice, we can pray anywhere.

The following pages will guide you through a session of prayer stages.

Something to think and pray about each day this
    week
The Presence of God
Freedom
Consciousness
The Word (leads you to the daily scripture and
    provides help with the text)

Conversation
Conclusion

It is most important to come back to these pages each day of the week as they are an integral part of each day's prayer and lead to the scripture and inspiration points.

Although written in the first person, the prayers are for "doing" rather than for reading out. Each stage is a kind of exercise or meditation aimed at helping you to get in touch with God and God's presence in your life. We hope that you will join the many people around the world praying with us in our sacred space.

The Presence of God

Bless all who worship you, almighty
God,
from the rising of the sun to its setting:
from your goodness enrich us,
by your love inspire us,
by your Spirit guide us,
by your power protect us,
in your mercy receive us,
now and always.

November 30 — December 6, 2014

Something to think and pray about each day this week:

Cloaked with Christ

Ignatius Loyola failed with at least two sets of companions before he settled on the small group who, with him, founded the Jesuits. His experience with his first followers was sobering. They were strong on enthusiasm and made the right spiritual noises, but they fell away when Ignatius was arraigned by the Inquisition, imprisoned, and humiliated. While Ignatius could see his experience as donning the livery of Christ, the young men who admired him were dismayed and felt something had gone wrong. So when Peter Faber, Francis Xavier, and others gathered round Ignatius in Paris, he held them off from any commitment until he had put them through the Spiritual Exercises, especially the meditation on "Two Standards," in which a person is invited to consider their personal choice to serve "under the standard," or banner, of Christ. They needed to taste the failure and hopelessness of the suffering Jesus, and maintain their faith and hope through it.

The Presence of God

Lord, help me to be fully alive to your holy presence.
Enfold me in your love.
Let my heart become one with yours.

Freedom

Many countries are at this moment suffering the agonies of war.
I bow my head in thanksgiving for my freedom.
I pray for all prisoners and captives.

Consciousness

At this moment, Lord, I turn my thoughts to you.
I will leave aside my chores and preoccupations.
I will take rest and refreshment in your presence Lord.

The Word

The Word of God comes down to us through the scriptures. May the Holy Spirit enlighten my mind and my heart to respond to the gospel teachings. (Please turn to your scripture on the following pages. Inspiration points are there should you need them. When you are ready, return here to continue.)

Conversation

Sometimes I wonder what I might say if I were to meet you in person, Lord.
I might say, "Thank You, Lord" for always being there for me.
I know with certainty there were times when you carried me,
When through your strength I got through the dark times in my life.

Conclusion

Glory be to the Father, and to the Son, and to the Holy Spirit,
As it was in the beginning, is now and ever shall be,
World without end. Amen.

Sunday 30th November,
First Sunday of Advent
Mark 13:33—37

Jesus said, "Beware, keep alert; for you do not know when the time will come. It is like a man going on a journey, when he leaves home and puts his slaves in charge, each with his work, and commands the doorkeeper to be on the watch. Therefore, keep awake—for you do not know when the master of the house will come, in the evening, or at midnight, or at cockcrow, or at dawn, or else he may find you asleep when he comes suddenly. And what I say to you I say to all: Keep awake."

- Jesus is speaking of his second coming at the end of time. But each of us, before that, can look forward to coming before our Lord. It means that we must so live that it does not matter when he comes.

- Our life becomes a preparation for the vision of happiness.

Monday 1st December
Matthew 8:5—11

When Jesus entered Capernaum, a centurion came to him, appealing to him and saying, "Lord, my servant is lying at home paralyzed, in terrible distress." And he said to him, "I will come and cure him." The centurion answered, "Lord, I am not worthy to have you come under my roof; but only speak the word, and my servant will be healed. For I also am a man under authority, with soldiers under me; and I say to one, 'Go,' and he goes, and to another, 'Come,' and he comes, and to my slave, 'Do this,' and the slave does it." When Jesus heard him, he was amazed and said to those who followed him, "Truly I tell you, in no one in Israel have I found such faith. I tell you, many will come from east and west and will eat with Abraham and Isaac and Jacob in the kingdom of heaven."

- Now, at the beginning of a new church year, we hear Jesus' mission statement or policy. The faith of a Roman soldier—a hated person for the local people—was the picture and sign of the coming of all nations into God's kingdom.

- Prayer humbles us to let us know that we are of these nations, getting into God's kingdom and love by his gracious gift and legacy, not by our own self-esteem or self-importance. Advent is the month of the humble God, the child who is God.

Tuesday 2nd December
Luke 10:22

At that same hour Jesus rejoiced in the Holy Spirit and said, "All things have been handed over to me by my Father; and no one knows who the Son is except the Father, or who the Father is except the Son and anyone to whom the Son chooses to reveal him."

- William Barclay writes: "We believe in evolution, the slow climb upward of man from the level of the beasts. Jesus is the end and climax of the evolutionary process, because in him man meets God; he is at once the perfection of manhood and the fullness of godhead."

**Wednesday 3rd December,
St. Francis Xavier
Matthew 15:29–37**

After Jesus had left that place, he passed along the Sea of Galilee, and he went up the mountain, where he sat down. Great crowds came to him, bringing with them the lame, the maimed, the blind, the mute, and many others. They put them at his feet, and he cured them, so that the crowd was amazed when they saw the mute speaking, the maimed whole, the lame walking, and the blind seeing. And they praised the God of Israel. Then Jesus called his disciples to him and said, "I have compassion for the crowd, because they have been with me now for three days and have nothing to eat; and I do not want to send them away hungry, for they might faint on the way." The disciples said to him, "Where are we to get enough bread in the desert to feed so great a crowd?" Jesus asked them, "How many loaves have you?" They said, "Seven, and a few small fish." Then ordering the crowd to sit down on the ground, he took the seven loaves and the fish; and after giving thanks he broke them and gave them to the disciples, and the disciples gave them to the crowds. And all of them ate and were filled; and they took up the broken pieces left over, seven baskets full.

- Jesus had compassion for the crowds. He sees me among them and knows my needs. I tell him where I am most challenged and listen for his word.

- Like Francis Xavier, I bring myself to the God who meets my needs for healing, strength, and encouragement. I listen for the words that God has for me.

Thursday 4th December
Matthew 7:21, 24–27

Jesus said to the people, "Not everyone who says to me, 'Lord, Lord,' will enter the kingdom of heaven, but only one who does the will of my Father in heaven. . . . Everyone then who hears these words of mine and acts on them will be like a wise man who built his house on rock. The rain fell, the floods came, and the winds blew and beat on that house, but it did not fall, because it had been founded on rock. And everyone who hears these words of mine and does not act on them will be like a foolish man who built his house on sand.

The rain fell, and the floods came, and the winds blew and beat against that house, and it fell—and great was its fall!"

- There are many ways to "hear" words. They can be just sound with practical content, like giving information or directions. The word of God is more like the word of a friend, spoken to the mind and to the heart.

- The Word of God gives meaning to life and is spoken always in love.

Friday 5th December
Matthew 9:27—31

As Jesus went on his way, two blind men followed him, crying loudly, "Have mercy on us, Son of David!" When he entered the house, the blind men came to him; and Jesus said to them, "Do you believe that I am able to do this?" They said to him, "Yes, Lord." Then he touched their eyes and said, "According to your faith let it be done to you." And their eyes were opened. Then Jesus sternly ordered them, "See that no one knows of this." But they went away and spread the news about him throughout that district.

- Can I imagine this scene where Jesus is walking along with two very noisy individuals pestering him?

- What happens? What is it like for them?

- Am I blind in any way? Can I put myself in this situation?

Saturday 6th December
Matthew 9:35—10:1, 6—8

Jesus went about all the cities and villages, teaching in their synagogues, and proclaiming the good news of the kingdom, and curing every disease and every sickness. When he saw the crowds, he had compassion for them, because they were harassed and helpless, like sheep without a shepherd. Then he said to his disciples, "The harvest is plentiful, but the laborers are few; therefore ask the Lord of the harvest to send out laborers into his harvest." Then Jesus summoned his twelve disciples and gave them authority over unclean spirits, to cast them out, and to cure every disease and every sickness. These twelve Jesus sent out with the following instructions: "Go rather to the lost sheep of the house of Israel. As you go, proclaim the good news, 'The kingdom of heaven has come near.' Cure the sick, raise the dead, cleanse the lepers, cast out demons. You received without payment; give without payment."

- Jesus cured every disease and sickness. I bring all aspects of my life to my prayer, knowing that God wants to bring healing, too.

- I may recall times when I have been too busy or too stressed. I picture Jesus looking with compassion on me then, keeping alive in his heart God's desire for me that I had lost sight of. I linger in Jesus' compassionate gaze.

The Second Week of Advent
December 7—13

Something to think and pray about each day this week:

Making Sense of Life

Scripture makes sense when it meets the non-scriptural world inside us. God works on us and touches us through experience and through scripture—the word of God. So in prayer, when we feel moved either by consolation or by disturbance, it is good to stop, to linger on the movement we feel. It is a theophany, a self-showing of God. We are on holy ground, as Moses sensed before the burning bush on Sinai. God is spirit, invisible, untouchable. But when we are alert, we can sense God's effect on us.

This can happen when we feel in utter desolation and reach outside ourselves: "There must be something beyond this." It can happen in communion and joy, like that of Peter at the Transfiguration: "This should go on forever; let the party never stop." It can happen in our places of prayer, during religious celebrations, in a park, or wherever we pray. In all cases, it is a gift, a grace, a promise, a lifting of the veil. For many devout people, the veil was seldom lifted. The great mystic John of the Cross wrote, "Love is the fruit of faith, that is to say, of darkness."

The Presence of God

God is with me, but more,
God is within me, giving me existence.
Let me dwell for a moment on God's life-giving presence
in my body, my mind, my heart, and in the whole of my life.

Freedom

God is not foreign to my freedom.
Instead the Spirit breathes life into my most intimate desires,
gently nudging me towards all that is good.
I ask for the grace to let myself be enfolded by the Spirit.

Consciousness

Help me, Lord, to be more conscious of your presence.

Teach me to recognize your presence in others.
Fill my heart with gratitude for the times your love
has been shown to me through the care of others.

The Word
I read the Word of God slowly, a few times
over, and I listen to what God is saying to me.
(Please turn to your scripture on the following
pages. Inspiration points are there should you
need them. When you are ready, return here to
continue.)

Conversation
How has God's Word moved me?
Has it left me cold?
Has it consoled me or moved me to act in a new
way?
I imagine Jesus standing or sitting beside me,
I turn and share my feelings with him.

Conclusion
Glory be to the Father, and to the Son, and to
the Holy Spirit,
As it was in the beginning, is now and ever shall be,
World without end. Amen.

Sunday 7th December,
Second Sunday of Advent
Mark 1:4–6

John the baptizer appeared in the wilderness, proclaiming a baptism of repentance for the forgiveness of sins. And people from the whole Judean countryside and all the people of Jerusalem were going out to him, and were baptized by him in the river Jordan, confessing their sins. Now John was clothed with camel's hair, with a leather belt around his waist, and he ate locusts and wild honey.

- The attraction of John the Baptist is mysterious. People flocked to him, not to be flattered but to be told the truth.

- They listened because of what they saw, a man who was indifferent to the world's prizes, a man of minimal needs, who could not be bought by pleasures, comforts, or money, but was passionate about God. They recognized holiness.

- Show me, Lord, what there is about my life that takes from the value of my words and makes me less convincing.

Monday 8th December,
The Immaculate Conception
of the Blessed Virgin
Luke 1:26–38

In the sixth month the angel Gabriel was sent by God to a town in Galilee called Nazareth, to a virgin engaged to a man whose name was Joseph, of the house of David. The virgin's name was Mary. And he came to her and said, "Greetings, favored one! The Lord is with you." But she was much perplexed by his words and pondered what sort of greeting this might be. The angel said to her, "Do not be afraid, Mary, for you have found favor with God. And now, you will conceive in your womb and bear a son, and you will name him Jesus. He will be great, and will be called the Son of the Most High, and the Lord God will give to him the throne of his ancestor David. He will reign over the house of Jacob forever, and of his kingdom there will be no end." Mary said to the angel, "How can this be, since I am a virgin?" The angel said to her, "The Holy Spirit will come upon you, and the power of the Most High will overshadow you; therefore the child to be born will be holy; he will be called Son of God. And now, your relative Elizabeth in her old age has also conceived a son; and this is the sixth month for her who was said to be barren. For nothing will be impossible with God." Then Mary said, "Here am I, the servant of the Lord; let it be with me according to your word." Then the angel departed from her.

- Mary held no special office. She was powerless: young in a world that valued age, female in a world ruled by men, poor in a stratified economy. So her being "favored" by God to be the mother of the long-awaited Messiah would have seemed to people in Jesus' time as a complete reversal of expectations.

- By responding positively to God's messenger, Mary becomes the model believer, servant and disciple, responding wholeheartedly to God's plan of salvation. Do I ever model myself on Mary in my response to God's call?

Tuesday 9th December
Matthew 18:12—14

J esus said to his disciples: "What do you think? If a man has a hundred sheep, and one of them has gone astray, does he not leave the ninety-nine on the hills and go in search of the one that went astray? And if he finds it, truly I say to you, he rejoices over it more than over the ninety-nine that never went astray. So it is not the will of my father who is in heaven that one of these little ones should perish."

- We are the little ones; all we are and have is from God who wants us to be at our best, our most alive. God wants nothing good in us to perish. Nothing good we have done or have tried to do is wasted. All is valued in the mind and heart of God, and we are saved, honoured, and loved by the one who creates us each day.

- Advent reminds us of what it is like to be a little one, dependent on others and on God for so much in life.

Wednesday 10th December
Matthew 11:28—30

Jesus said, "Come to me, all you that are weary and are carrying heavy burdens, and I will give you rest. Take my yoke upon you, and learn from me; for I am gentle and humble in heart, and you will find rest for your souls. For my yoke is easy, and my burden is light."

- Let us sit a while with this precious and familiar text. Do I hear Jesus speak these words to me?

- How do I respond now?

Thursday 11th December
Matthew 11:11—15

Jesus said to the crowds, "Truly I tell you, among those born of women no one has arisen greater than John the Baptist; yet the least in the kingdom of heaven is greater than he. From the days of John the Baptist until now the kingdom of heaven has suffered violence, and the violent take it by force. For all the prophets and the law prophesied until John came; and if you are willing to accept it, he is Elijah who is to come. Let anyone with ears listen!"

- John may be the greatest figure of the past, but, from Jesus' perspective—now that the Messiah has appeared—whoever believes in Jesus and accepts his teaching about God's kingdom is greater than John. But Jesus remains entwined with John the Baptist, as he does with Elijah, as well as with the apostles and the women who follow him.

- In the same way, we are entwined with Jesus, and with all those who are part of the journey with Jesus to God.

Friday 12th December
Matthew 11:16—19

J esus spoke to the crowds, "But to what will I compare this generation? It is like children sitting in the marketplaces and calling to one another, 'We played the flute for you, and you did not dance; we wailed, and you did not mourn.' For John came neither eating nor drinking, and they say, 'He has a demon'; the Son of Man came eating and drinking, and they say, 'Look, a glutton and a drunkard, a friend of tax collectors and sinners!' Yet wisdom is vindicated by her deeds."

24

- Jesus compares his generation to children playing "make believe" games. Some refuse to play the wedding game ('we piped for you') while others refuse to play the funeral game ('you did not mourn').

- Do I play games with God so that I can remain undisturbed, and maintain my lifestyle no matter what it does to others, especially the poor and the excluded?

Saturday 13th December
Matthew 17:10–13

And the disciples asked him, "Why, then, do the scribes say that Elijah must come first?" He replied, "Elijah is indeed coming and will restore all things; but I tell you that Elijah has already come, and they did not recognize him, but they did to him whatever they pleased. So also the Son of Man is about to suffer at their hands." Then the disciples understood that he was speaking to them about John the Baptist.

- Elijah was one of the great prophets in Israel. Jesus is saying that John the Baptist is the new Elijah because he has acted as Jesus' prophetic forerunner. But just as people did not believe John, and he was put to death, so they do not believe Jesus, who will also be put to death.

- Jesus suffered primarily because he claimed to be God's son. Am I prepared to suffer for my Christian faith when people mock my beliefs, or do I simply accommodate myself to the values of those around me?

The Third Week of Advent
December 14—20

Something to think and pray about each day this week:

Seeking God
Jesus shows how to find goodness where others see only bad. The prime example is the father of the prodigal son. Once the boy has turned towards home, the father falls on his neck and throws a party. The party is neither for the son nor for the rest of the family. It is the father expressing his own joy; it is his party: "There is more joy among the angels in heaven over one sinner. . . ." Jesus urges us to be perfect in this way, going the extra mile, generous to a fault. It is a counsel of perfection, rare in this world, but when it happens, God is shown.

The Presence of God
What is present to me is what has a hold on my becoming.
I reflect on the presence of God always there in love,

amidst the many things that have a hold on me.
I pause and pray that I may let God affect my
becoming in this precise moment.

Freedom

"There are very few people who realize what
God
would make of them if they abandoned themselves into his hands,
and let themselves be formed by his grace" (St.
Ignatius).
I ask for the grace to trust myself totally to God's
love.

Consciousness

In the presence of my loving Creator,
I look honestly at my feelings over the last day,
the highs, the lows, and the level ground.
Can I see where the Lord has been present?

The Word

God speaks to each one of us individually. I
need to listen to hear what he is saying to me.
Read the text a few times, then listen. (Please
turn to your scripture on the following pages.

Inspiration points are there should you need them. When you are ready, return here to continue.)

Conversation

What is stirring in me as I pray?
Am I consoled, troubled, left cold?
I imagine Jesus himself standing or sitting at my side,
and share my feelings with him.

Conclusion

Glory be to the Father, and to the Son, and to the Holy Spirit,
As it was in the beginning, is now and ever shall be,
World without end. Amen.

Sunday 14th December,
Third Sunday of Advent
John 1:6—8, 19—28

There was a man sent from God, whose name was John. He came as a witness to testify to the light, so that all might believe through him. He himself was not the light, but he came to testify to the light. This is the testimony given by John when the Jews sent priests and Levites from Jerusalem to ask him, "Who are you?" He confessed and did not deny it, but confessed, "I am not the Messiah." And they asked him, "What then? Are you Elijah?" He said, "I am not." "Are you the prophet?" He answered, "No." Then they said to him, "Who are you? Let us have an answer for those who sent us. What do you say about yourself?" He said, "I am the voice of one crying out in the wilderness, 'Make straight the way of the Lord,'" as the prophet Isaiah said. Now they had been sent from the Pharisees. They asked him, "Why then are you baptizing if you are neither the Messiah, nor Elijah, nor the prophet?" John answered them, "I baptize with water. Among you stands one whom you do not know, the one who is coming after me; I am not worthy to untie the thong of his sandal." This took place in Bethany across the Jordan where John was baptizing.

- We are in the atmosphere of something about to happen. John the Baptist is still on the scene, pointing where to look, where to wait, how to expect the one who is to come. We get so used to Christmas and the coming of Christ that we hardly have any sense of expectation.

- Christmas is not meant to be quiet. It's meant to draw out many responses in us. This could be a week of active expectancy—to do something to prepare well for the Lord. How will you prepare for Christmas?

Monday 15th December
Matthew 21:23—27

When Jesus entered the temple, the chief priests and the elders of the people came to him as he was teaching, and said, "By what authority are you doing these things, and who gave you this authority?" Jesus said to them, "I will also ask you one question; if you tell me the answer, then I will also tell you by what authority I do these things. Did the baptism of John come from heaven, or was it of human origin?" And they argued with one another, "If we say, 'From heaven,' he will say to us, 'Why then did you not believe him?' But if we say, 'Of human origin,' we are afraid of the crowd; for all regard John as a prophet." So they answered Jesus, "We do not know." And he said to them, "Neither will I tell you by what authority I am doing these things."

- Jesus does not engage in futile discussion. There are times when words may get in the way, when no amount of speech will help.

- Am I sometimes like the priests and elders? Quizzing, figuring out, arguing, debating? Jesus values a faith that is lively, engaged, generous, and uncomplicated. I spend time with Jesus, careful not to be always talking and quizzing.

Tuesday 16th December
Matthew 21:28–32

J esus said, "What do you think? A man had two sons; he went to the first and said, 'Son, go and work in the vineyard today.' He answered, 'I will not'; but later he changed his mind and went. The father went to the second and said the same; and he answered, 'I go, sir'; but he did not go. Which of the two did the will of his father?" They said, "The first." Jesus said to them, "Truly I tell you, the tax collectors and the prostitutes are going into the kingdom of God ahead of you. For John came to you in the way of righteousness and you did not believe him, but the tax collectors and the prostitutes believed him; and even after you saw it, you did not change your minds and believe him."

- Jesus speaks this parable to me. I avoid applying it to others right now and simply accept Jesus' warmth as he sees how I have served. I listen for his invitation as he shows me where I hold back.

- To live in the kingdom is to be ready to rub shoulders with all kinds. God's love is given freely and is accepted by many. I pray for a heart that is open to those who are not like me.

Wednesday 17th December
Matthew 1:1—11

An account of the genealogy of Jesus the Messiah, the son of David, the son of Abraham. Abraham was the father of Isaac, and Isaac the father of Jacob, and Jacob the father of Judah and his brothers, and Judah the father of Perez and Zerah by Tamar, and Perez the father of Hezron, and Hezron the father of Aram, and Aram the father of Aminadab, and Aminadab the father of Nahshon, and Nahshon the father of Salmon, and Salmon the father of Boaz by Rahab, and Boaz the father of Obed by Ruth, and Obed the father of Jesse, and Jesse the father of King David. And David was the father of Solomon by the wife of Uriah, and Solomon the father of Rehoboam, and Rehoboam the father of Abijah, and Abijah the father of Asaph, and Asaph the father of Jehoshaphat, and Jehoshaphat the father of Joram, and Joram the father of Uzziah, and Uzziah the father of Jotham, and Jotham the father of Ahaz, and Ahaz the father of Hezekiah, and Hezekiah the father of Manasseh, and Manasseh the father of Amos, and Amos the father of Josiah, and Josiah the father of Jechoniah and his brothers, at the time of the deportation to Babylon.

- Matthew's gospel opens with a genealogy to place Jesus' birth within the context of Jewish history from the time of Abraham. Alongside the patriarchs, kings, and unknowns are four women, all outsiders: Tamar, Rahab, Ruth, and Bathsheba, each with a marital history that contained elements of human scandal. In this way Matthew prepares his readers for the extraordinary way in which Jesus was conceived, and Mary's place in this history.

• God writes not in copperplate but with crooked lines. Lord, help me recognize my role in spreading the good news.

Thursday 18th December
Matthew 1:18–25

Now the birth of Jesus the Messiah took place in this way. When his mother Mary had been engaged to Joseph, but before they lived together, she was found to be with child from the Holy Spirit. Her husband Joseph, being a righteous man and unwilling to expose her to public disgrace, planned to dismiss her quietly. But just when he had resolved to do this, an angel of the Lord appeared to him in a dream and said, "Joseph, son of David, do not be afraid to take Mary as your wife, for the child conceived in her is from the Holy Spirit. She will bear a son, and you are to name him Jesus, for he will save his people from their sins." All this took place to fulfill what had been spoken by the Lord through the prophet: "Look, the virgin shall conceive and bear a son, and they shall name him Emmanuel," which means, "God is with us." When Joseph awoke from sleep, he did as the angel of the Lord commanded him; he took her as his wife.

• There is a model here for making decisions and dealing with doubts. Pray about it, carry it as a question, pester God about it. This is the story of Joseph's utterly unique vocation, as foster-father of the Son of God.

Friday 19th December
Luke 1:5—25

In the days of King Herod of Judea, there was a priest named Zechariah, who belonged to the priestly order of Abijah. His wife was a descendant of Aaron, and her name was Elizabeth. Both of them were righteous before God, living blamelessly according to all the commandments and regulations of the Lord. But they had no children, because Elizabeth was barren, and both were getting on in years. Once when he was serving as priest before God and his section was on duty, he was chosen by lot, according to the custom of the priesthood, to enter the sanctuary of the Lord and offer incense. Now at the time of the incense-offering, the whole assembly of the people was praying outside. Then there appeared to him an angel of the Lord, standing at the right side of the altar of incense. When Zechariah saw him, he was terrified; and fear overwhelmed him. But the angel said to him, "Do not be afraid, Zechariah, for your prayer has been heard. Your wife Elizabeth will bear you a son, and you will name him John. You will have joy and gladness, and many will rejoice at his birth, for he will be great in the sight of the Lord. He must never drink wine or strong drink; even before his birth he will be filled with the Holy Spirit. He will turn many of the people of Israel to the Lord their God. With the spirit and power of Elijah he will go before him, to turn the hearts of parents to their children, and the disobedient to the wisdom of the righteous, to make ready a people prepared for the Lord." Zechariah said to the angel, "How will I know that this is so? For I am an old man, and my wife is getting on in years." The angel replied, "I am Gabriel. I stand in the presence of God, and I have been sent to speak to you and to bring you this good news. But now, because you did not believe my words, which will be fulfilled in their time, you will become mute, unable to speak, until the day these things occur." Meanwhile, the people were waiting for Zechariah, and wondered at his delay in the sanctuary. When he did come out, he could not speak to them, and they realized that he had seen a vision in the sanctuary. He kept motioning to them and remained unable to speak. When his time of service was ended, he went to his home. After those days his wife Elizabeth conceived, and for five months she remained in seclusion. She said, "This is what the Lord has done for me when he looked favorably on me and took away the disgrace I have endured among my people."

• Zechariah was speechless through lack of faith. His obstinacy to belief made him like a remote island.

• But Zechariah was never deserted by God; with the birth of John his faith returned and God looked favorably on him. A child may often bring us to faith where faith is missing.

- Watch a child today, think of a child today, remember childhood today; and be close to life, to mystery, and to God!

Saturday 20th December
Isaiah 7:10—14

Again the Lord spoke to Ahaz, saying, "Ask a sign of the Lord your God; let it be deep as Sheol or high as heaven." But Ahaz said, "I will not ask, and I will not put the Lord to the test." Then Isaiah said: "Hear then, O house of David! Is it too little for you to weary mortals, that you weary my God also? Therefore the Lord himself will give you a sign. Look, the young woman is with child and shall bear a son, and shall name him Immanuel."

- "Emmanuel"—a mantra for Advent and Christmas prayer. If we speak it from the heart, we are in touch with the mystery of the God who is near, close to the God who is present in our hearts. God is as near as the air we breathe.

- With each breath in prayer, just say "Emmanuel." This is our Christmas welcome to the child who is our God.

The Fourth Week of Advent/Christmas
December 21—27

Something to think and pray about each day this week:

The Joy of Waiting

This last week of Advent is a time of waiting—and that has its own pleasures: for children, perhaps the sound of Dad's car on the drive, the key turning in the front door. Anticipation is a joy, and at Christmas the Eve is often better than the indulgence of the Day. Our preparation is for a guest. Life—and human history—is not just one thing after another. God broke in on human history two thousand years ago and nothing is the same since. The world is young though it may feel old. Christmas is a birthday. We survive on the bright spots, when things are special: light at the end of the tunnel. Advent is the tunnel, and it used to have its share of fasting and repentance, sharpening the contrast between anticipation and Event.

In what sense does God arrive at Christmas? In Innsbruck they re-enact the arrival, putting a live baby and mother on a sleigh drawn through the lighted town. That is lovely but imaginary. The real arrival is partly in our hearts, partly in our Mass. True, that happens more than once a year. But on this feast, as on a birthday, we celebrate that Bethlehem event which showed (as birthday presents show), that we are the children God wanted, that we matter to him.

The Presence of God
God is with me, but more, God is within me.
Let me dwell for a moment on God's life-giving presence
in my body, in my mind, in my heart,
as I sit here, right now.

Freedom
"A thick and shapeless tree-trunk would never believe
that it could become a statue, admired as a miracle of sculpture,
and would never submit itself to the chisel of the sculptor,
who sees by her genius what she can make of it."
(St. Ignatius)

I ask for the grace to let myself be shaped by my loving Creator.

Consciousness
Knowing that God loves me unconditionally,
I can afford to be honest about how I am.
How has the last day been, and how do I feel now?
I share my feelings openly with the Lord.

The Word
I read the Word of God slowly, a few times over, and I listen to what God is saying to me. (Please turn to your scripture on the following pages. Inspiration points are there should you need them. When you are ready, return here to continue.)

Conversation
Do I notice myself reacting as I pray with the Word of God?
Do I feel challenged, comforted, angry?
Imagining Jesus sitting or standing by me, I speak out my feelings,
as one trusted friend to another.

Conclusion

Glory be to the Father, and to the Son, and to
the Holy Spirit,
As it was in the beginning, is now and ever shall
be,
World without end. Amen.

Sunday 21st December,
Fourth Sunday of Advent
Luke 1:26—38

In the sixth month the angel Gabriel was sent by God to a town in Galilee called Nazareth, to a virgin whose name was Mary. And he came to her and said, "Greetings, favored one! The Lord is with you." But she was much perplexed by his words and pondered what sort of greeting this might be. The angel said to her, "Do not be afraid, Mary, for you have found favor with God. And now, you will conceive in your womb and bear a son, and you will name him Jesus. He will be great, and will be called the Son of the Most High, and the Lord God will give to him the throne of his ancestor David. He will reign over the house of Jacob forever, and of his kingdom there will be no end." Mary said to the angel, "How can this be, since I am a virgin?" The angel said to her, "The Holy Spirit will come upon you, and the power of the Most High will overshadow you; therefore the child to be born will be holy; he will be called Son of God. And now, your relative Elizabeth in her old age has also conceived a son; and this is the sixth month for her who was said to be barren. For nothing will be impossible with God." Then Mary said, "Here am I, the servant of the Lord; let it be with me according to your word." Then the angel departed from her.

- Christmas highlights the belief that God is in all of us. We can ignore that, or we can help God be found in all of us. God is active through each of us for each other.

- In the visit of Mary, God came close to Elizabeth in the ordinary and homely moments of every day. These Advent and Christmas days give us the space to allow the huge, eternal mystery to become part of the everyday.

Monday 22nd December
Luke 1:46—56

And Mary said, "My soul magnifies the Lord, and my spirit rejoices in God my Savior, for he has looked with favor on the lowliness of his servant. Surely, from now on all generations will call me blessed; for the Mighty One has done great things for me, and holy is his name. His mercy is for those who fear him from generation to generation. He has shown strength with his arm; he has scattered the proud in the thoughts of their hearts. He has brought down the powerful from their thrones, and lifted up the lowly; he has filled the hungry with good things, and sent the rich away empty. He has helped his servant Israel, in remembrance of his mercy, according to the promise he made to our ancestors, to Abraham and to his descendants forever." And Mary remained with Elizabeth about three months and then returned to her home.

- Having heard that her son is to be the son of David and Son of God, Mary translates this into good news for the lowly and hungry people of the world and a warning for the rich and powerful. Her *Magnificat* demonstrates what God will do: he will scatter the arrogant, pull down the mighty, send the rich away empty, exalt the lowly, fill the hungry, and lead his people by the hand. This is the reversal that Jesus announces in the Beatitudes.

- Do I find myself on the side of the lowly or, without openly admitting it, on the side of the arrogant?

Tuesday 23rd December
Luke 1:57–66

Now the time came for Elizabeth to give birth, and she bore a son. Her neighbors and relatives heard that the Lord had shown his great mercy to her, and they rejoiced with her. On the eighth day they came to circumcise the child, and they were going to name him Zechariah after his father. But his mother said, "No; he is to be called John." They said to her, "None of your relatives has this name." Then they began motioning to his father to find out what name he wanted to give him. He asked for a writing tablet and wrote, "His name is John." And all of them were amazed. Immediately his mouth was opened and his tongue freed, and he began to speak, praising God. Fear came over all their neighbors, and all these things were talked about throughout the entire hill country of Judea. All who heard them pondered them and said, "What then will this child become?" For, indeed, the hand of the Lord was with him.

• When the people turn to the dumb Zechariah, they watch him writing on a tablet, confirming what his wife has said. At that very moment, his power of speech returns and he starts to praise God. They are in awe, and the whole affair becomes a talking point throughout the hill country of Judea as people wonder what the future holds for baby John.

- With any birth, we may wonder what the future holds for the little baby. As I look back on my own life, what have I become?

Wednesday 24th December
Luke 1:67—79

Then his father Zechariah was filled with the Holy Spirit and spoke this prophecy: "Blessed be the Lord God of Israel, for he has looked favorably on his people and redeemed them. He has raised up a mighty savior for us in the house of his servant David, as he spoke through the mouth of his holy prophets from of old, that we would be saved from our enemies and from the hand of all who hate us. Thus he has shown the mercy promised to our ancestors and has remembered his holy covenant, the oath that he swore to our ancestor Abraham, to grant us that we, being rescued from the hands of our enemies, might serve him without fear, in holiness and righteousness before him all our days. And you, child, will be called the prophet of the Most High; for you will go before the Lord to prepare his ways, to give knowledge of salvation to his people by the forgiveness of their sins. By the tender mercy of our God, the dawn from on high will break upon us, to give light to those who sit in darkness and in the shadow of death, to guide our feet into the way of peace."

- Every day, this prayer of Zechariah becomes the morning prayer of thousands of people across the world. I read it slowly, letting the words reveal their meaning for me today.

- Zechariah is profoundly aware of his heritage, seeing God's action in the past as having promise for the future. I draw encouragement from my own story, allowing God to bless me with hope and confidence in continued blessing.

Thursday 25th December, Feast of the Nativity of the Lord
Luke 2:1—14

In those days a decree went out from Emperor Augustus that all the world should be registered. This was the first registration and was taken while

Quirinius was governor of Syria. All went to their own towns to be registered. Joseph also went from the town of Nazareth in Galilee to Judea, to the city of David called Bethlehem, because he was descended from the house and family of David. He went to be registered with Mary, to whom he was engaged and who was expecting a child. While they were there, the time came for her to deliver her child. And she gave birth to her firstborn son and wrapped him in bands of cloth, and laid him in a manger, because there was no place for them in the inn. In that region there were shepherds living in the fields, keeping watch over their flock by night. Then an angel of the Lord stood before them, and the glory of the Lord shone around them, and they were terrified. But the angel said to them, "Do not be afraid; for see—I am bringing you good news of great joy for all the people: to you is born this day in the city of David a Savior, who is the Messiah, the Lord. This will be a sign for you: you will find a child wrapped in bands of cloth and lying in a manger." And suddenly there was with the angel a multitude of the heavenly host, praising God and saying,

"Glory to God in the highest heaven, and on earth peace among those whom he favors!"

- Luke tells us about some shepherds who live in the fields and watch their flocks by night. The scribes and Pharisees would have regarded these men as ritually unclean, as "outsiders." Luke mentions them to give encouragement to all those who lacked status in society, and for whom Jesus had a special regard.

- In Luke's story, Mary and Joseph are portrayed as transients, somewhat like "the homeless" of our contemporary city streets. Are such people in my thoughts and concerns this Christmas?

Friday 26th December,
St. Stephen, the First Martyr
Acts 7:54—59

When those in the synagogue heard these things, they became enraged and ground their teeth at Stephen. But filled with the Holy Spirit, he gazed into heaven and saw the glory of God and Jesus standing at the right hand of God. "Look," he said, "I see the heavens opened and the Son of Man standing at the right hand of

God!" But they covered their ears, and with a loud shout all rushed together against him. Then they dragged him out of the city and began to stone him; and the witnesses laid their coats at the feet of a young man named Saul. While they were stoning Stephen, he prayed, "Lord Jesus, receive my spirit." Then he knelt down and cried out in a loud voice, "Lord, do not hold this sin against them." When he had said this, he died. And Saul approved of their killing him.

- Violence already, and on the morning after the birthday of the Prince of Peace! Such an horrific occasion, when men who call themselves god-fearing take up stones to kill Stephen.

- All through history, people have yielded to the temptation to use violence in this way, but it is in the name of a god of their own creation.

- Lord, teach me to turn towards you; even as you did with Saul who looked on at this murder, and approved.

Saturday 27th December,
St. John, Evangelist
John 20:1—8

So Mary Magdalene ran and went to Simon Peter and the other disciple, the one whom Jesus loved, and said to them, "They have taken the Lord out of the tomb, and we do not know where they have laid him." Then Peter and the other disciple set out and went toward the tomb. The two were running together, but the other disciple outran Peter and reached the tomb first. He bent down to look in and saw the linen wrappings lying there, but he did not go in. Then Simon Peter came, following him, and went into the tomb. He saw the linen wrappings lying there, and the cloth that had been on Jesus' head, not lying with the linen wrappings but rolled up in a place by itself. Then the other disciple, who reached the tomb first, also went in, and he saw and believed.

- John links the end of Jesus' passion and death with the new life of the resurrection: Christmas with Easter. All of our prayer is from this side of Easter. We are the ones who know by faith that the Christ child is the risen Lord. Christmas is the feast of glory, the glory of God hidden in the child who would rise from death.

December 28, 2014 — January 4, 2015

Something to think and pray about each day this week:

Into the New Year

Lord, this has been another difficult year across the globe. As it slips away in these last few days, I pray about what has happened to me, and to my world, since last January. How was I touched by the great events of the year? Have I become more compassionate, or more selfish and defensive? It seems that year after year there are momentous events, in nature, business, and government. We could easily droop with depression, crying in the old Gaelic lament, "*Ochón agus ochón agus ochón!*"

Success is what we do with our failures. Somewhere in all this misery, Lord, you have a lesson for us. We do not learn it if we simply circle the wagons and defend the way we have always been. We have seen the consequences of unbridled greed. As we wish one another a happy new year, we might think twice before adding "and prosperous." The blinkered pursuit of prosperity has not spread happiness wider. Teach me, Lord.

The Presence of God
As I sit here, the beating of my heart,
the ebb and flow of my breathing,
the movements of my mind
are all signs of God's ongoing creation of me.
I pause for a moment, and become aware of this
presence of God within me.

Freedom
I ask for the grace to let go of my own concerns
and be open to what God is asking of me,
to let myself be guided and formed by my loving
Creator.

Consciousness
In the presence of my loving Creator,
I look honestly at my feelings over the last day,
the highs, the lows, and the level ground.
Can I see where the Lord has been present?

The Word
I take my time to read the Word of God,
slowly, a few times, allowing myself to dwell on

anything that strikes me. (Please turn to your scripture on the following pages. Inspiration points are there should you need them. When you are ready, return here to continue.)

Conversation
Remembering that I am still in God's presence,
I imagine Jesus himself standing or sitting beside me,
and say whatever is on my mind, whatever is in my heart,
speaking as one friend to another.

Conclusion
Glory be to the Father, and to the Son, and to the Holy Spirit,
As it was in the beginning, is now and ever shall be,
World without end. Amen.

Sunday 28th December,
The Holy Family
Luke 2:41—52

Now every year his parents went to Jerusalem
for the festival of the Passover. And when
he was twelve years old, they went up as usual for
the festival. When the festival was ended and they
started to return, the boy Jesus stayed behind in
Jerusalem, but his parents did not know it. Assuming
that he was in the group of travelers, they went
a day's journey. Then they started to look for him
among their relatives and friends. When they did
not find him, they returned to Jerusalem to search
for him. After three days they found him in the
temple, sitting among the teachers, listening to
them and asking them questions. And all who
heard him were amazed at his understanding and
his answers. When his parents saw him they were
astonished; and his mother said to him, "Child,
why have you treated us like this? Look, your
father and I have been searching for you in great
anxiety." He said to them, "Why were you searching
for me? Did you not know that I must be in
my Father's house?" But they did not understand
what he said to them.

- I imagine that I'm young and I live near Joseph's house; he and Mary often invite me to come over, and they welcome me. I love to be there, and to play with their son, their child.

- Let me sit with my thoughts, with what I feel in this moment.

Monday 29th December
Luke 2:25—32

Now there was a man in Jerusalem whose name was Simeon; this man was righteous and devout, looking forward to the consolation of Israel, and the Holy Spirit rested on him. It had been revealed to him by the Holy Spirit that he would not see death before he had seen the Lord's Messiah. Guided by the Spirit, Simeon came into the temple; and when the parents brought in the child Jesus, to do for him what was customary under the law, Simeon took him in his arms and praised God, saying, "Master, now you are dismissing your servant in peace, according to your word; for my eyes have seen your salvation, which you have prepared in the presence of all peoples, light for revelation to the Gentiles and for glory to your people Israel."

- Simeon's prayer, the night prayer of the Church, invites us to let go of conflict, disappointment, and loss; of all that keeps us from God and from living life to the full. We live in the light of God's promise to grace us with the light of peace, joy, and security.

- Even in times of unhappiness, confusion, and lack of faith, the love and peace of God are near. Our heart "sees" the salvation and the loving presence of God in prayer, in service, and in love.

Tuesday 30th December
Luke 2:36—40

There was also a prophet, Anna the daughter of Phanuel, of the tribe of Asher. She was of a great age, having lived with her husband for seven years after her marriage, then as a widow to the age of eighty-four. She never left the temple but worshipped there with fasting and prayer night and day. At that moment she came, and began to praise God and to speak about the child to all who were looking for the redemption of Jerusalem. When they had finished everything required by the law of the Lord, they returned to Galilee, to their own town of Nazareth. The child grew and became strong, filled with wisdom; and the favor of God was upon him.

- Mary, Joseph, and their baby return to their hometown of Nazareth, and Luke tells us, "the child grew and became strong, filled with wisdom." In order to be the model for his disciples, Jesus had to be fully human. Jesus learned step-by-step, as every human must: how to lace his sandals, how to react to skinned knees, and what it meant to be Jesus of Nazareth and Son of God.

- What does all this tell me about my image of Jesus?

Wednesday 31st December
John 1:1—5

In the beginning was the Word, and the Word was with God, and the Word was God. He was in the beginning with God. All things came into being through him, and without him not one thing came into being. What has come into being in him was life, and the life was the light of all people. The light shines in the darkness, and the darkness did not overcome it.

- John's gospel opens with a Prologue, a hymn that sums up his view of who Jesus was. John asserts, in opposition to the synagogue leaders, that Jesus was a divine being. In trying to explain what he meant, he drew on ideas from the Old Testament that spoke of God's Word. From John's point of view, Jesus was God's Word spoken to the people of Israel.

- At his birth, Jesus was truly God, but he no longer knew it. In the same way, each of us is born male or female, but it takes us a long time to grasp even a hazy understanding of what that means. So it was with Jesus. Just as with each one of us, his lifetime was a series of new insights into who he was.

Thursday, 1st January,
Solemnity of Mary, Mother of God
Luke 2:16—20

So they went with haste and found Mary and Joseph, and the child lying in the manger. When they saw this, they made known what had been told them about this child; and all who heard it were amazed at what the shepherds told them. But Mary treasured all these words and pondered them in her heart. The shepherds returned, glorifying and praising God for all they had heard and seen, as it had been told them.

- We are named and loved by God before birth. From the moment of conception, we are named in the mind and love of God just as Jesus was. We carry that love through life.

- In prayer you might repeat your baptismal—or "Christian"—name like a mantra, and allow God's choice of you to fill that name with thanks, love, and commitment.

- Happy New Year!

Friday 2nd January
John 1:19—28

This is the testimony given by John when the Jews sent priests and Levites from Jerusalem to ask him, "Who are you?" He confessed and did not deny it, but confessed, "I am not the Messiah." And they asked him, "What then? Are you Elijah?" He said, "I am not." "Are you the prophet?" He answered, "No." Then they said to him, "Who are you? Let us have an answer for those who sent us. What do you say about yourself?" He said,

"I am the voice of one crying out in the wilderness, 'Make straight the way of the Lord,'" as the prophet Isaiah said. Now they had been sent from the Pharisees. They asked him, "Why then are you baptizing if you are neither the Messiah, nor Elijah, nor the prophet?" John answered them, "I baptize with water. Among you stands one whom you do not know, the one who is coming after me; I am not worthy to untie the thong of his sandal." This took place in Bethany across the Jordan where John was baptizing.

- John the Baptist knew there was little he could do himself, on his own. The one to come was the one all were waiting on. John's life was dependent on Jesus for meaning.

- We are not self-made, but are all God-made, at the beginning of life and all during our lives. Let me pray about this.

Saturday 3rd January
John 1:35—39

The next day John saw Jesus coming toward him and declared, "Here is the Lamb of God who takes away the sin of the world! This is he of whom I said, 'After me comes a man who ranks ahead of me because he was before me.' I myself did not know him; but I came baptizing with water for this reason, that he might be revealed to Israel." And John testified, "I saw the Spirit descending from heaven like a dove, and it remained on him. I myself did not know him, but the one who sent me to baptize with water said to me, 'He on whom you see the Spirit descend and remain is the one who baptizes with the Holy Spirit.' And I myself have seen and have testified that this is the Son of God."

- This is the culminating moment of John's life, the arrival of the One for whom he prepared the way.

- Can I hear John's account of himself? He knew he was to prepare the way, but until now, he didn't know the identity of the one he was preparing for.

- How do I understand John? Does he move me to look towards the one who was to come?

Sunday 4th January,
The Epiphany of the Lord
Matthew 2:1—2, 7—12

In the time of King Herod, after Jesus was born in Bethlehem of Judea, wise men from the East came to Jerusalem, asking, "Where is the child who has been born king of the Jews? For we observed his star at its rising, and have come to pay him homage." Herod secretly called for the wise men and learned from them the exact time when the star had appeared. Then he sent them to Bethlehem, saying, "Go and search diligently for the child; and when you have found him, bring me word so that I may also go and pay him homage." When they had heard the king, they set out; and there, ahead of them, went the star that they had seen at its rising, until it stopped over the place where the child was. When they saw that the star had stopped, they were overwhelmed with joy. On entering the house, they saw the child with Mary his mother; and they knelt down and paid him homage. Then, opening their treasure chests, they offered him gifts of gold, frankincense, and myrrh. And having been warned in a dream not to return to Herod, they left for their own country by another road.

- Can you remember some time in life when you were overcome with joy?

- Joy is a gift from God and a share in the nature of God, for God is joy. Allow this joy to be part of your life and part of your prayer this day. Allow the tough times to find their place there, too.

Introduction to the Advent Retreat

Welcome to our Advent Retreat. A retreat is always an invitation from God—an invitation to set out on a journey, a journey with no path and a destination as yet unknown. This journey will bring us into the depths of our own being; it will confront and challenge our prejudices—the attitudes we have inherited from tradition, culture, family, peer group and society, and the programmed ways of behaving within which those attitudes have imprisoned us. This journey—if entered into with an open mind and open heart—will help us to get to know ourselves better; and in getting to know ourselves better, we get to know God better, because God is to be found in the deepest desires of our heart.

The invitation to start out on this journey is always received as a challenge: a challenge to leave our comfort zones and our securities—particularly the securities of our set ways of thinking—in order to move closer to the God who loves us. The one thing that is certain as we start on this journey is that we do not know where that challenge will come from or where it will lead us. Even if we resist the challenge because part of us wants to stay where we are, God will never give up inviting us to come closer. To accept the invitation and move, without fear, into the unknown, we need to be rooted in the infinite and unconditional love of God for us. We are surrounded by that love of God, as in a thick fog, and it penetrates to the very core of our being. No matter what happens to us, no matter even how we may have offended God, this love never dissipates. Rooted in this sense of security, we can move forward and leave our other securities behind.

Suggestions

This retreat is divided into four meditations. St. Ignatius, when directing a retreat, never allowed the person on retreat to know what was coming ahead: he wanted them to concentrate on the meditation in hand, to focus on the here and now, and so he only gave them what they required for the here and now. While all four meditations and reflections are included here, I would suggest that you follow the advice of St. Ignatius and not read ahead. Stay with the first meditation until you are finished, and only then move on to the next.

Each person will have a different approach to a retreat: some may choose to spend a full day covering all four meditations; others may divide them over four days; others again may wish to use one meditation for each week of Advent and spend some time each day on that meditation, to savour it and allow it to sink deeper into their hearts.

Before you start the first meditation, decide how long you wish to pray for. Some may be comfortable staying in prayer before God for a full hour; others may find that too much, and decide on thirty minutes, or twenty minutes. Whatever you decide, St. Ignatius would ask you to be faithful to that time, even if you find it difficult, distracting, dry, or feel you are getting nowhere. We are not praying in order to get nice feelings or fresh insights. We can at least offer to God the time we have allocated to prayer, and leave God to do the rest. After each meditation, spend a few minutes reflecting on what happened during your time of prayer. Write down any thoughts that struck you and whatever feelings you experienced. To

First Moment of Prayer

Preparation

Settle down into a comfortable position, but not *too* comfortable—you need to stay awake! Breathe deeply several times. Concentrate on your breathing, and imagine all your worries, distractions, and other concerns falling away. As you breathe in, reflect that this breath is yet another gift given to you by God in love, and give thanks for this new gift; as you breathe out, reflect that you want to give yourself to God and ask God for the generosity to do so as completely as possible.

Read the following passage slowly. Pause after every few lines or at phrases that touch you. Repeat such phrases several times, allowing them to sink into your heart.

Matthew 6:25–33

Therefore I tell you, do not worry about your life, what you will eat or what you will drink, or about your body, what you will wear. Is not life more than food, and the body more than clothing? Look at the birds of the air; they neither sow nor reap nor gather into barns, and yet your heavenly Father feeds them. Are you not of more value than they? And can any of you by worrying add a single hour to your span of life? And why do you worry about clothing? Consider the lilies of the field, how they grow; they neither toil nor spin, yet I tell you, even Solomon in all his glory was not clothed like one of these. But if God so clothes the grass of the field, which is alive today and tomorrow is thrown into the oven, will he not much more clothe you—you of little faith? Therefore do not worry, saying, "What will we eat?" or "What will we drink?" or "What will we wear?" For it is the Gentiles who strive for all these things; and indeed your heavenly Father knows that you need all these things. But strive first for the kingdom of God, and his righteousness, and all these things will be given to you as well.

Background

The early Christian communities were having enormous problems: those Christians who had converted from Judaism were under a lot of pressure to return to their Jewish faith: their families disowned them, their community ostracised them, their employers sacked them, and in the new

Christian community that they had joined, they suffered persecution as well as possible arrest and execution. The communities were also often poor, struggling to make ends meet, but what they had, they shared. Many wondered if they had made a big mistake joining this new community.

As they listened to this gospel being read at their Sunday assembly, they were reminded of the love and care that God has for them; they were encouraged to keep going despite all the difficulties they experienced, because God was looking after them and would never let them down.

Picture
Imagine two people madly in love, locked in an embrace that they wish would never end. Each thinking only of the other, not concerned for themselves. This is how God loves you. Perhaps this is what eternity will be like, God's never-ending embrace of love.

Prayer
Ask God to help you to experience his infinite, unconditional love for you and never to doubt it.

Meditation

Your imagination is a gift from God. Use it now to help you pray.

Imagine yourself sitting amongst the crowd, listening to Jesus. Maybe you are in a field, or perhaps a town square. Look around at the crowd who is listening intently to Jesus speaking. Then turn your eyes to Jesus. Watch him as he talks. Look into his eyes. Imagine his eyes looking down at you. Listen to him speaking. As he speaks, imagine that he is looking at you intently, as if no one else was present. He is addressing you. Allow yourself to pause at any words or phrases that touch you, repeating them again and again, allowing them to sink into your heart and enjoy the love of God that they express for you, for love is always to be enjoyed.

After Meditation

Spend a few minutes reflecting on what happened during your time of prayer.

- Write down any thoughts that struck you and any feelings you experienced.

- What does the passage tell you about who God is?

- Does the passage challenge any attitudes you have?

- Does it have any relevance to the way you live?

- Advent is typically a time of many preparations; how do Jesus' words about trust fit with the mood of the season?

- Good news is proclaimed to the poor; how do you receive it? How might you announce it?

- How do you seek the kingdom and strive for the reign of God this Advent?

Reflection

The sage often invited believers to see how their god reflected their own personal qualities. If you are a loving, gentle, generous, forgiving kind of person, you will see your god has similar qualities, he would point out. If you are hot-tempered, angry, vengeful, and authoritarian, you will see your god is likewise. You are known by the god you believe in, he would conclude; your god is a mirror that reflects you to yourself.

—*The Ocean in the Dewdrop*
Francis J. Padinjarekara

Second Moment of Prayer

Preparation

Settle down into a comfortable position. Breathe deeply several times. Concentrate on your breathing, and feel all your worries, distractions, and other concerns falling away. As you breathe in, feel yourself being filled with the love that God has for you; the deeper the breath, the more you will feel filled with God's love. As you breathe out, offer yourself to God and ask God to show you the path to love.

Read the following passage slowly. Pause after every few lines or at phrases that touch you. Repeat such phrases several times, allowing them to sink into your heart.

Matthew 25: 31—40

When the Son of Man comes in his glory, and all the angels with him, then he will sit on the throne of his glory. All the nations will be gathered before him, and he will separate people one from another as a shepherd separates the sheep from the goats, and he will put the sheep at his right hand and the goats at the left. Then the king will say to those at his right hand, "Come, you that are blessed by my Father, inherit the kingdom prepared for you from the foundation of the world; for I was hungry and you gave me food, I was thirsty and you gave me something to drink, I was a stranger and you welcomed me, I was naked and you gave me clothing, I was sick and you took care of me, I was in prison and you visited me."

Then the righteous will answer him, "Lord, when was it that we saw you hungry and gave you food, or thirsty and gave you something to drink? And when was it that we saw you a stranger and welcomed you, or naked and gave you clothing? And when was it that we saw you sick or in prison and visited you?" And the king will answer them, "Truly I tell you, just as you did it to one of the least of these who are members of my family, you did it to me."

Background

Jesus came to proclaim the coming of the Kingdom of God. The early Christian community understood that their community was the seed from which the Kingdom of God would grow until it reached its perfection. Then Jesus would return again and hand it over to the Father. As they listened to this passage being read at the Sunday assembly, they understood Jesus to be talking about the sort of place that the Kingdom of God is like and therefore they understood Jesus to be telling them how their community should be living; this passage reminded them of who God is and of what was important to God.

Picture

Imagine a family in Pakistan or Benin who has lost everything in the floods; or a homeless young person living on the street wondering where they will sleep tonight, or where they can get something to eat; or a young woman being abused by her violent husband.

Imagine God looking down on that family or person. Reflect that God loves them also with the same infinite love with which God loves you. Try to imagine what God is thinking or feeling (to use human concepts, as we have no other concepts to use!) as God watches their suffering.

Prayer

Ask God to help you understand what God is asking from you. You were created for a purpose; you have a specific role to play in the building of the Kingdom of God. Ask God to help you to be faithful to that role.

Meditation

Imagine the scene: every human being ever created standing before Jesus. Imagine yourself amongst them. Listen to Jesus speaking. Imagine that Jesus has you in mind as he speaks. Re-read the passage again, very slowly. Listen to the gratitude in his voice. Feel the love that Jesus is expressing for you. Pause at any words or phrases that touch you, repeating them again and again, allowing them to sink into your heart. Allow the passage to inform you of who God is and what God wants.

After Meditation

Spend a few minutes reflecting on what happened during your time of prayer.

- Write down any thoughts that struck you and any feelings you experienced.

- What does the passage tell you about who God is?

- Does the passage challenge any attitudes you have?

- Does it have any relevance to the way you live?

- Jesus is concerned with those who hunger, thirst, are naked or in prison; how are his priorities reflected in how you spend Advent?

Reflection

A sincere seeker said: "I have always longed to see God everywhere and in all things, and live in God's presence. I have practised it but I haven't succeeded." "This isn't something you bring about by practice," the sage replied. "When you understand who you are, you'll no longer seek God's presence—you'll realise that you are God's presence."

—*The Ocean in the Dewdrop*
Francis J. Padinjarekara

Third Moment of Prayer

Preparation

Settle down into a comfortable position. Breathe deeply several times. Concentrate on your breathing. Try to leave all your worries and other concerns aside while you give this time to prayer. As you breathe in, you are receiving—literally—the gift of life from God; as you breathe out, you are offering that life, which you have been freely given, back to God for God to use as God wishes.

Read the following passage slowly. Pause after every few lines or at phrases that touch you. Repeat such phrases several times, allowing them to sink into your heart.

Matthew 9:10–14

As Jesus sat at dinner in the house, many tax collectors and sinners came and were sitting with him and his disciples. When the Pharisees saw this, they said to his disciples, "Why does your teacher eat with tax collectors and sinners?" But when he heard this, he said, "Those who are well have no need of a physician, but those who are sick. Go and learn what this means, 'I desire mercy, not sacrifice.' For I have come to call not the righteous but sinners."

Luke 15:1—2

Now all the tax collectors and sinners were coming near to listen to him. And the Pharisees and the scribes were grumbling and saying, "This fellow welcomes sinners and eats with them."

Background

These passages talk about Jesus eating. For us, this is a description of an ordinary event in the life of Jesus. But for the early Christian community, it meant something of enormous importance. The early Christian community understood that Jesus was the Son of God and often described the Kingdom of God as a feast, at which God presides. So when they heard this passage being read at the Sunday assembly—Jesus eating with tax collectors and sinners—it brought to mind the Kingdom of God, where Jesus reigns. They understood that those who were unwanted and rejected here on earth would be God's close friends and companions in the Kingdom of God. Everyone is a child of God and has the dignity of being a child of God, and no one can take that away from them. As the early Christian community understood itself to be the seed from which would grow the Kingdom of God, they heard these passages as instructions as to how the community should live together— welcoming, accepting, and open to those whom society wants nothing to do with.

Picture
Imagine a beggar coming up towards you, unkempt, unshaven, maybe even smelling. Imagine him standing right in front of you. You can smell his breath—not very pleasant. His hands are outstretched towards you. He is not asking for money, he is asking for your companionship.

Prayer
Ask God to open your mind and heart to help you understand what God is saying to you in this passage.

Meditation
Imagine the scene, Jesus and a group of people sitting down together to share a meal. Imagine Jesus and his companions talking and laughing together. Imagine people passing by, complaining of the

company he was keeping. Re-read the passages again, very slowly. Pause at any words or phrases that touch you, repeating them again and again, allowing them to sink into your heart. Allow the passages to inform you of who God is and what God wants.

After Meditation

Spend a few minutes reflecting on what happened during your time of prayer.

- Write down any thoughts that struck you and any feelings you experienced.

- What does the passage tell you about who God is?

- Does the passage challenge any attitudes you have?

- Does it have any relevance to the way you live?

- Do your Advent and Christmas meals reflect the meals that Jesus enjoyed?

Reflection

A social worker who had spent many years working for her local community said: "I have gone out of my way to help people, but I find no gratitude. There is little more than selfishness in people."

The sage's comment: "Where judgments end, happiness begins."
> —*The Ocean in the Dewdrop*
> Francis J. Padinjarekara

Fourth Moment of Prayer

Preparation

Settle down into a comfortable position. Breathe deeply several times. Focus on the present moment: you, breathing in and out. The past is gone, the future has not yet arrived, the only reality that exists is you breathing in and out, being loved by God, in this present moment.

Matthew 24:42—47

"Keep awake therefore, for you do not know on what day your Lord is coming. But understand this: if the owner of the house had known in what part of the night the thief was coming, he would have stayed awake and would not have let his house be broken into. Therefore you also must be ready, for the Son of Man is coming at an unexpected hour. Who then is the faithful and wise slave, whom his master has put in charge of his household, to give the other slaves their allowance of food at the proper time? Blessed is that slave whom his master will find at work when he arrives.

Truly I tell you, he will put that one in charge of all his possessions."

Background
The early Christian community was expecting Jesus to return in glory very soon and bring the Kingdom of God, already present in the community, to its final glorious fulfillment. However, as time went on and there was no sign of Jesus returning, some began to doubt and felt tempted to give up. This passage was intended as an encouragement to the community to persevere and not waiver from the path on which, at the invitation of Jesus, they had embarked.

Picture
Imagine someone running a marathon. He has almost completed the course, but his legs are feeling the strain. He wonders if he can finish the race. Someone comes up and runs alongside him, telling him how well he has run so far and urging him to keep going the last mile and finish what he has begun.

Prayer

Ask God to help you understand what God is saying to you in this passage.

Meditation

Jesus is addressing the disciples. Imagine yourself amongst them. You are there, right up close to Jesus, as he speaks. Jesus understands their weariness, their constant efforts to follow him. He is sympathetic to those who feel the effort is too much. Re-read the passage above, very slowly. Pause at any words or phrases that touch you, repeating them again and again, allowing them to sink into your heart. Allow the passage to inform you of who God is and what God wants.

After Meditation

Spend a few minutes reflecting on what happened during your time of prayer.

- Write down any thoughts that struck you and any feelings you experienced.

- What does the passage tell you about who God is?

- Does the passage challenge any attitudes you have?

- What do you need to stay awake to this Advent?

Reflection

A man had traveled by train from a faraway place. On the way, his suitcase was stolen. When he arrived, he had nothing more than the clothes he was wearing. He was disturbed and angry, as he sat listening to the sage. After his dialogue with the sage, he said: "My suitcase was just a suitcase until it was stolen. Now it has become a precious lesson in letting go."

—*The Ocean in the Dewdrop*
Francis J. Padinjarekara

Founded in 1865, Ave Maria Press,
a ministry of the Congregation of
Holy Cross, is a Catholic publishing
company that serves the spiritual and
formative needs of the Church and its
schools, institutions, and ministers;
Christian individuals and families; and
others seeking spiritual nourishment.

—————◆—————

For a complete listing of titles from

Ave Maria Press

Sorin Books

Forest of Peace

Christian Classics

visit www.avemariapress.com

ave maria press® / Notre Dame, IN 46556
A Ministry of the United States Province of Holy Cross